Dr.

Overcoming Anxiety in Teens and Pre-Teens: A Parent's Guide

by Dr. Richard L. Travis

Thank You for purchasing this book.

"Overcoming Depression in Teens and Pre-Teens: A Parent's Guide"

Printed and bound in the United States
Copyright © 2012 by Dr. Richard L. Travis

All rights reserved. This book or any portion thereof may not be reproduced or used in any manner whatsoever without the express written permission of the publisher except for the use of brief quotations in a book review or scholarly journal.

First Printing: 2014
ISBN-13: 978-1495211577
ISBN-10: 1495211576

RLT Publishing
www.rltpublishing.com

Ordering Information:
Special discounts are available on quantity purchases by corporations, associations, educators, and others. For details, contact the publisher at the above listed address.

U.S. trade bookstores and wholesalers:
Please Visit: **www.drrichardtravis.com/**

Introduction:

This book is dedicated to all of those parents who have suffered through temper tantrums, mood swings, shouting matches, pouting, and arguments with their children. Please do not consider yourself a failure if your child is depressed or anxious. The challenge, as it always is with parents, is how to manage your time and help your child.

The challenge is also to gather all the information together that you can, and create an "action plan" to help create an environment which will aid your child in dealing with, and perhaps conquering this anxiety, and grow into a healthy adult.

This book is going to open your eyes on the topic of anxiety and other related mental disorders. I'm sure the term "mental disorders" is a frightening one. It is a term that is used for the diagnosis of an emotional problem that is actually a clinical problem, and not just "normal anxiety," or even just growing pains. You will be able to walk away from reading this book with the knowledge that either your child needs clinical help (a medical evaluation) for the treatment of anxiety, or that you just need TIPS to deal with the behaviors of that age group.

You will be able to make an "action plan" for your child, which will make life in your home more manageable and peaceful, and give new tools to your child to deal with life more effectively.

You will easily be able to identify your role in your child's development, socially and perhaps even genetically. You are encouraged to not only read this book, but take ownership of your own stress levels in dealing with your child. De-stress and deal with the issues your children bring to the table with a sense of calm and composure, and you will have greater success. Good Luck!

*****The Reading of this book should not be used at the exclusion of seeking professional help, if professional help has been suggested.

Table of Contents

Introduction: 3
What is Anxiety? 7
Causes of Anxiety 7
    Genetic Predisposition 7
    Environmental Influences 8
    Other Associations 8
How does Anxiety Manifest? 9
Manifestations Based On Age 9
    Anxiety in Preteens 9
    Anxiety in Teenagers 11
Manifestations Based on Gender 15
    How does anxiety show up in boys? 15
    Anxiety in Girls 17
Classifications of Childhood and Teenager Anxiety 19
    Generalized Anxiety Disorder (GAD) 19
    Panic Disorder 19
    Obsessive Compulsive Disorder (OCD) 20
    Social Phobia 20
    Other Phobias 21
    Post-Traumatic Stress Disorder (PTSD) 21
    Separation Anxiety Disorder 22
    Selective Mutism 23
Diagnosis of Anxiety 24
Complications of Untreated Anxiety 27

Treatment of Anxiety Disorder in Pre-Teens and Teenagers 29
- Holistic Therapy 29
- Modalities of Holistic Therapy for Anxiety 30
- Other Calming Exercises for Children 35
- Physical exercises for children 37
- Indications for Holistic Therapy 39
- Contraindications of Holistic Therapy 40
- Cognitive-Behavioral Therapy 40
- Advantages of CBT 41
- Disadvantages of CBT 42

Medical Treatment of Childhood and Teenage Anxiety ... 43
- Facts about Anxiety Medications 43
- Drugs Treating Childhood and Teenage Anxiety 44
- Classification of Anti-Anxiety Drugs 44
- Antihistamines 49
- Beta-Blockers 50
- Benzodiazepines 53
- Treatment of Withdrawal Syndrome Symptoms 59
- Other Anti-Anxiety Medications 61

Hints for Parents and Caretakers 63
Conclusion 67
Links 69
- Other Books and E-Books in Dr. T's Living Well Series: . 71
- Information about the Author: 81

What is Anxiety?

Anxiety is defined as a feeling of extreme fear, nervousness, uneasiness or worry of impending doom, or of an event of undetermined outcome. However, <u>anxiety is not always a pathological process.</u> The same feeling occurs normally in association with an intense desire to do something. Every child or teenager experiences some degree of anxiety as part of their normal social and emotional development. Anxiety becomes a problem when it is prolonged and starts to interfere with the normal expected daily activities of the child or teenager. Normal anxiety responds to comfort and reassurance; this is not true with pathological anxiety.

Causes of Anxiety

The causes of anxiety are multi-factorial, meaning that some children are genetically predisposed, while others acquire anxiety from their thoughts or the stimulation of the surrounding environment.

Genetic Predisposition

Some children and teenagers inherit the feelings of anxiety from either of their parents. If it runs in the family, then the probability of having an anxious child diagnosed with clinical anxiety increases with the number of siblings. These children tend to develop anxiety symptoms early in their lives as babies or toddlers, and anxiety worsens with progressing age.

Environmental Influences

The environmental influences on the development of anxiety differ with age. The sources of anxiety for young babies and toddlers may be people strange to them, loud disturbing noises, heights and separation from their parents. For preschool children, loneliness is the major cause of anxiety, but darkness may cause it as well. When a child ages, anxiety responses shift to academics, supernatural beings, socialization, tests, criticism, and physical trauma. They are overly afraid of failure, social situations, ghosts and threats. In older children and adolescents, the focus turns to less-specific fears, such as impending war, political catastrophe and social and family relationships.

As a child grows up, family changes such as the coming of new siblings, parental conflicts and separation, loss of an elderly grandparent and shifting homes can all trigger an anxiety response. Traumatic experiences, such as death of a sibling or a peer, illness of the child or a close family member, or parental abuse are additional sources of childhood anxiety. In extreme conditions, especially in conflict prone areas, community violence and humanitarian crises present a growing child with conditions too harsh for them to handle.

Other Associations

Anxiety in children and teenagers may not occur as an isolated condition. Other mental conditions such as Attention Deficit/Hyperactivity Disorder (ADHD), Major Depressive Disorder, and eating disorders could be coexisting with the anxiety. These disorders are usually more severe, and should be ruled out in any child or teenager with diagnosed anxiety.

How does Anxiety Manifest?

In order to manifest signs and symptoms of anxiety, children and teenagers have to imagine scenarios. Research has shown that children start having an active imagination at approximately eight years old. This does not mean that young children and babies do not get anxious. As mentioned above, anxiety can be characterized by fear, nervousness, uneasiness, worry and panic, among other things, depending on age. In addition, anxiety manifestations also differ in terms of gender and will be discussed later.

Manifestations Based On Age

Anxiety in Preteens

In babies and toddlers, the major form of anxiety is fear. Some mothers and caretakers may ignore these signs as either normal or just a passive phase of development. This can be catastrophic as the child ages.

> Crying- This is the most common manifestation of anxiety in a young child. Children cry when they are hungry or in pain and they calm down when these problems are taken care of. A child who is restless, highly irritable and always sad without identifiable cause could be anxious.

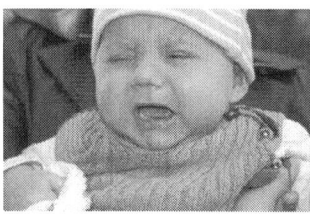 

Figure 1: *(A) An anxious child crying uncontrollably as a manifestation of anxiety disorder, (B) while the other crying and clinging to her mother.*

Eating disturbances- At different points in a child's life eating can be a problem, but this problem fades away sooner or later. Protracted difficulties in eating, such as refusing food, crying while being fed, or keeping food in the mouth or regurgitating it, are all signs of anxiety. For those able to talk, poor appetite is the main complaint.

Figure 2: *Anxiety may manifest with eating disorders in both preteens and teenagers*

Sleeping difficulties- Children usually sleep longer than adults, and more deeply so. A child who cannot easily fall asleep and stay asleep is described as an insomniac. Some may sleep only to be awakened by nightmares and terrors. These are telltale signs of anxiety that are easier to spot in older children and early teenagers.

Figure 3: *Childhood insomnia*

Excessive clinginess- Children who suffer anxiety because of fear of separation may manifest excessive clinginess, and will not want to be on their own. When they are carried, they tend to hold tight, and any attempt to free them makes the grip even tighter. There also may be crying associated with this clinginess.

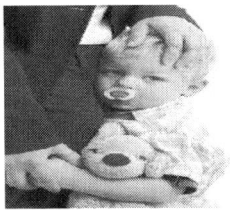

Figure 4: *children who suffer from anxiety often cling to their parents to get confidence to face their fears.*

Anxiety in Teenagers

Anxiety is more severe in teenagers compared to preteens, and can be much more easily recognized. This is because these children are active socially and academically, and so anxiety effects are seen in many areas of their lives.

Withdrawal- Children suffering from anxiety are usually withdrawn from other family members, as well as their daily activities. They seem not to enjoy playing with the rest, or engaging in discussions or interacting with peers. This is a very reliable sign of anxiety, but depression should not be overlooked also. Some children suffer from social phobia, manifesting as extreme shyness and lack of confidence while in front of or addressing others. This a variant of anxiety, but can also occur as an independent condition.

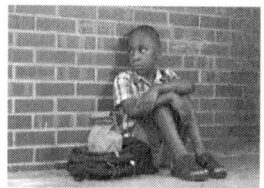 

Figure 5: *Image of an anxious child and a teenager manifesting withdrawal as a sign of anxiety.*

Concentration problems- Normal children can concentrate on activities for long periods of time without getting bored. This is not true with anxious children and teenagers. This lack of concentration has a profound effect on their performance, which begin to decline despite help from teachers and parents. The lack of concentration is further worsened with poor memory.

Figure 6: *Lack of concentration is major manifestation of anxiety*

Physical complaints- Anxious teenagers often complain of pain without an identifiable cause. The symptoms are usually nonspecific; ranging from pains such as headaches and stomach aches, to generalized body weakness, manifesting as fatigue and malaise present at rest. These pains do not respond to medication, as opposed to those of organic origin.

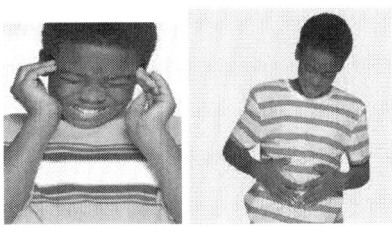

Figure 7: *Young boys suffering from somatic symptoms of headache and stomach ache.*

Isolation or Avoidance- Anxious teenagers tend to avoid certain places or things, or refuse to do things or go places. This is because they associate these situations with undetermined outcomes. Forcing the teenagers to do things they are afraid of can lead to serious complications.

Figure 8: *An anxious child isolates himself and avoids the company of peers.*

Negative behaviors- These teenagers are overly pessimistic, only entertaining negative thoughts with nothing positive to look up to. They concentrate on and exaggerate negatives, always imagining the worst outcomes. In addition, anxious teenagers criticize themselves for mistakes they are not responsible for, always feeling guilty, as well as inflexible and rigid.

Temperamental behaviors- A frowning face, agitation, anger, restlessness, aggression, easy irritability, defiance and opposition to authorities define an anxious teenager. This interferes with their relationship with peers, teachers or parents. Any attempts to punish the defiance, opposition or aggression can worsen the anxiety in these teenagers.

Skepticism and perfectionism- Anxious teenagers are skeptical of performing their tasks and always seek perfection. They fear failure, and so they procrastinate a great deal before doing anything. They often become greatly disappointed if they fall short of their objectives.

Constant worry- These teenagers are at all times worried about what might happen, or they are dwelling on what has already happened.

Figure 6: *An image of a constantly worried patient*

Manifestations Based on Gender

How does anxiety show up in boys?

Research has shown that boys tend to have more severe forms of anxiety disorders, especially attention deficit/hyperactivity disorder. It has been erroneously thought that more females suffer then males.

- Young boys who suffer from anxiety tend to be more irritable and temperamental compared to their female counterparts.

- Adolescent males and teenagers with anxiety, manifest opposition to authorities, which can cause problems between them and other friends or family, as well as teachers at school. Attempts to punish this behavior tend to worsen the anxiety.

- Anxious teenagers often entertain suicidal thoughts. Girls tend to be more affected with these thoughts than boys, but boys are more likely to carry out their threat, and actually make an attempt to kill themselves. This means that an anxious girl will think of committing suicide, but is less likely to go ahead and try it, while an anxious teenage boy will more likely attempt suicide.

- Anxious teenage boys are more likely to turn to alcohol and other substances of abuse in order to relieve their anxiety, as compared to their female counterparts. Thus if a teenage boy starts abusing alcohol, then one possibility is that he is masking an anxiety disorder. Of course peer pressure is a major cause of alcohol consumption by teens.

- Some forms of anxiety disorders manifest more clearly in male children and teenagers than in females. For example generalized anxiety disorder, social phobias, and acute panic attacks are more common in males.

Anxiety in Girls

Girls are considered to be more predisposed to developing anxiety, and at a younger age. This however has not been proven scientifically by research. The fact of the matter is that anxiety occurs equally in male and female teenagers. This misconception arises from the fact that females are more likely to openly talk about their issues, while males hide or indulge in activities that help mask their anxious moments. These are the manifestations of anxiety in girls:

- Anxious girls tend to manifest excessive crying, which seems purposeless and unprovoked. This is the initial sign of anxiety in a young girl.

- Girls are more predisposed to develop obsessive compulsive disorder (OCD) compared to their male counterparts, and this can be severe enough to interfere with their relationships with peers.

- Most girls are constantly worried and openly discuss their feelings. This is a fact that makes it easier for them to be put into treatment for anxiety disorder.

- Anxious female girls not only suffer more severe forms of social phobia, but also other phobias including the fear of objects, heights, travel, and animals among other things.

- Withdrawal is more prominent in girls than boys. This may be because girls are more playful, and any slight reduction in their level of activity is noticed easily.

- Somatic symptoms or complaints, such as painful body parts, stomach aches and headaches are seen with anxious girls more than boys. Some pains are severe enough to warrant hospital visits, and even attempts at medical treatment.

- Girls or teenagers suffering from anxiety may manifest other symptoms such as perfectionism and skepticism.

Classifications of Childhood and Teenager Anxiety

Based on the manifestations of anxiety in preteens and teenagers, anxiety can be classified into eight classes or disorders depending on the predominant manifestation. These classes may influence the treatment option for the condition. They are discussed below;

Generalized Anxiety Disorder (GAD)

This form of anxiety is characterized by excessive worry and panic on a variety of issues, ranging from school grades, peer relationships, perceived family problems and performance in sport activities. These children would do anything to achieve perfection, and constantly seek to be approved and reassured by peers and family members.

Figure 9: A child with generalized anxiety disorder.

Panic Disorder

These are sudden reactions of anxiety and panic occurring at least twice consecutively, followed by at least another thirty days of worry about having other similar attacks. These children and teenagers are overly stressed, and worried to the point of fear of losing their minds.

Figure 10: *Acute panic attack in a teenager*

Obsessive Compulsive Disorder (OCD)

This form of anxiety disorder is characterized by a serious preoccupation with certain thoughts (obsessions), and a strong desire to oftentimes repeat certain habits and routines (compulsions) in order to relieve the anxiety. These obsessions and compulsions greatly interfere with their social interactions and relationship with the environment. For example, they may be obsessed with hygiene and order, making it impossible to live with others who the anxious child will always consider untidy and disorganized.

Social Phobia

Also known as social anxiety disorder, present in children and teenagers as extreme fear of social situations, such as being called upon to address the class, or just starting up a conversation with a peer at school or in the neighborhood. Children with social phobia cannot start and maintain relationships with peers and school mates. In addition, this phobia interferes with their performance in school and sport activities.

Figure 11: An anxious child suffering social phobia

Other Phobias

Apart from the social phobia, children may also manifest other specific forms of anxiety. These include an agonizing dread of certain objects, such as insects, or situations such as traveling and flying, that would otherwise seem harmless to normal children. Common sources of childhood fears are certain animals, heights, water, medical equipment, blood and darkness. Children will try to avoid situations or objects that they dread. If they cannot, they endure them, but with a lot of anxiety, which can manifest with inconsolable crying, irritability, restlessness and agitation.

Post-Traumatic Stress Disorder (PTSD)

Although many children undergo traumatic experiences, not all of them progress to develop PTSD. Most of these children recover completely in a short period of time with comfort and reassurance. A small number of these children however, become intensely fearful, anxious, apprehensive, highly irritable and emotionally silent. They will try as much as possible to avoid situations, places, individuals or activities associated with or leading to the traumatic or life-threatening experience they had.

Those children most likely to develop post-traumatic stress disorder are those who witness the event directly, or were involved either by getting injured or losing a parent or a sibling. In addition, children who had a pre-existing history of mental health disturbance before the traumatic episode, as well as those who experience family violence, are also at increased risk.

Separation Anxiety Disorder

Almost all children between eighteen months to three years of age experience the anxiety of separating from their parents when the parents leave them alone. Most children are usually successfully distracted from these anxious feelings, but some never grow out of it. This kind of anxiety is normal, and also occurs at the time the child joins a daycare center. It manifests by crying, which usually resolves itself as the child gets acclimatized to the new surroundings and the people.

The problem arises when a child seems to take longer to be calmed after separation compared to other children of a similar age, or even older. These children have the abnormal (or pathological) form of anxiety and need treatment. They are extremely anxious while away from home, appearing withdrawn, overly worried and sad.

Figure 12*: A child suffering separation anxiety*

Such children will refuse to attend school, campsites or sleepovers despite reassurance from family, because of fear and separation. Any attempts to force them to do something might worsen the anxiety and can be met with misery and agony. In their young minds, the children imagine bad things happening to their loved ones in their absence, but cannot do anything to help them.

Selective Mutism

These children choose to remain silent in situations they would normally be expected to speak, as in school or while playing with peers. This greatly interferes with their performance in school and their ability to make friends. In order to diagnose selective mutism, it must be proven that the child talks normally at home or while around those he or she is comfortable. In most cases parents of these children actually get surprised by the teachers report that the child is abnormally quiet in school. Children with this form of anxiety tend to manifest it at the age of four to eight years old, or when they start schooling.

Diagnosis of Anxiety

In order to come up with the correct diagnosis of an anxiety disorder, the doctor may need to ask certain questions which only the parents or the caretaker of the children and teenagers would know. Other questions are specific to the child. Diagnosis involves taking a complete history and performing a physical examination of the patient. Parents are therefore required to be attentive every time they are with their children, in order to identify unusual behaviors manifested by their children. Among the things a doctor may want to know include:

- The duration of the symptoms or the presenting complaints.

- The chronology of the child or teenager's physical, emotional as well as intellectual development.

- Situations associated or contributing to anxious episodes.

- The extent to which the symptoms interfere with the child or teenager's daily activities.

- Any efforts that have been made in an attempt to alleviate anxiety.

- Any family member both immediate and extended who has ever had such symptoms.

- History of exposure to any stressful situation such as trauma, accident, death of a close relative or a parent or family problems.

Answers to the above questions can give an idea as to the causes and the classification of the anxiety disorder from which the child or teenager is suffering. Thus the mother, father or caretaker providing information should be as candid and as honest as possible in order not to miss any of the information necessary to make the correct diagnosis.

Many other conditions, some very dangerous, can be masked by anxiety. Therefore the doctor seeing the anxious child or teenager must try as much as possible to uncover any of these conditions. In this situation, relief of anxiety may actually be dangerous, because the underlying disease may be lethal if masked. Each of the anxiety disorders has its own criteria of diagnosis, most of which are clinical.

- **Generalized Anxiety Disorder**: Excessive, uncontrollable worry about many issues that would ordinarily be forgotten by children shortly after they happen may characterize this disorder. Examples are: upcoming events, previous conversations, sports or academic performances, family and personal health, and global events.

- **Acute Panic Attacks**: Characterized by extreme fearfulness, racing and pounding heartbeats, shortness of breath, lightheadedness and dizziness, uncontrolled shaking and trembling, and intense worry about losing one's mind or life.

- **Obsessive Compulsive Disorder**: Endless worry leading to the preoccupation to do something repeatedly, with the belief that if it is not done something harmful, deadly, or seriously wrong could happen. Preoccupations include cleanliness, extreme organization, and certain behaviors in order to keep away some of the thoughts causing anxiety.

- **Social phobia**: These children are excessively afraid of situations subjecting them to social scrutiny; such as having to address a class, or perform in front of peers. A diagnosis is given after a complete history is taken, as the child or teenager will confess an extreme fear of embarrassing, humiliating or ridiculing situations. Adolescents present with refusal to go to school and somatic (physical complaints), such as stomach pains and headache.

- **Post-Traumatic Stress Syndrome**: This is based squarely on clinical evaluation and a history of stressful situations. These children normally have a history of horrific, terrifying and frightening experiences, which they re-experience, leading to emotional numbness and excessive arousal.

- **Separation Anxiety Disorder**: This occurs in young children when they have to leave their mother's bedrooms to sleep on their own and when they start schooling. It is easy to diagnose, as one only needs to watch the child's behavior during separation.

- **Selective mutism**: Diagnosis of this anxiety disorder is based on an observation of the child. Usually the child is seen to be abnormally quiet when he or she is expected to talk. They should also be observed to see if there are situations in which they do talk.

Complications of Untreated Anxiety

Anxiety in children and teenagers is expected as a normal part of development as a child interacts with the environment, and his or her social surrounding. Parents or caretakers might be responsible for some of the complications that develop as a result of untreated anxiety. Overprotective parents may cause their children to carry anxiety into adulthood with very unpleasant consequences. It is therefore very important to keenly observe a child or a teen for the above discussed behaviors, and deal with them before they progress.

Anxiety is highly debilitating and interferes with the normal daily lifestyle of the children and the teenagers. The possible complications are as follows:

• **Inability to achieve social and academic potential-** Anxious children and teenagers are unable to concentrate in class and have poor memories. These behaviors impact their academic performance. In addition, these children are usually withdrawn, and so are socially isolated, which interferes with their social development.

• **Loss of friendships and family relationships-** If childhood anxiety is not addressed early, these children and teenagers may end up being lonely and unable to relate to friends and family members.

• **Low self-esteem and inferiority complex-** These children and teenagers may end up as adults who are not self-confident and believe that they are never good in anything that they do, and that they are always second-best.

- **Suicidal tendencies-** This is the most feared complication of anxiety. Although very uncommon in childhood, it is more common in adolescents and older teenagers. Children and adolescents who are severely depressed and anxious may be so affected that they view ending their own lives as the ultimate solution to their problems. Research has shown that about forty percent of anxious adolescents have suicidal thoughts, and about half of these actually attempt suicide.

- **Increased tendencies for alcohol and substance abuse later in life-** Many adult alcoholics, smokers and substance abusers have a history of anxiety. Thus they indulge in these practices believing that they can solve their problems. This may have started in the teenage years for those with social phobias, as alcohol may have been used to boost confidence. There is great concern that this could lead to addiction and dependence. Heavy smoking and drug abuse in adolescents is highly related to childhood post-traumatic stress disorder.

- **Physical effects-** Constantly worried children may develop some of the most dreaded diseases in adulthood, such as heart failure, high blood pressure, gastric ulcers, cancers and inflammatory bowel disease (due to constant stomach aches).

- **Migraine, tension and cluster headaches-** Children with untreated anxiety tend to develop these forms of headaches as they age. These are seriously debilitating, and can interfere with performance in school and work.

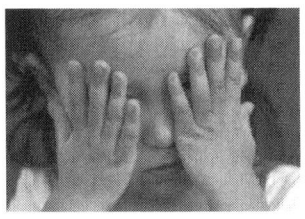

Treatment of Anxiety Disorder in Pre-Teens and Teenagers

As discussed above, anxiety disorders in childhood and teenage years can be quite problematic if left untreated. There are two treatment modalities used by pediatric psychiatrists and psychologists to help children and teenagers cope with anxiety; these are cognitive-behavioral therapy and psychotropic medications. Cognitive-behavioral therapy has scientifically been proven to work as do medications. Using either one of the two modalities is less effective, but a combination therapy is what is recommended by most doctors. In addition to these two modalities, holistic therapy has also been proven to be effective.

Holistic Therapy

Anxiety involves the physical, spiritual and mental aspects of a child's or a teenager's life. Therefore the holistic approach has been used successfully to treat some cases of anxiety. In holistic therapy, the process aims to heal the whole aspect of the child, focusing on positive behavior modification and the use of certain spiritual and physical practices.

Modalities of Holistic Therapy for Anxiety

Massage Therapy:

Pediatric massage therapy involves touching in a special way, certain superficial parts of the body and even deeper muscle layers, to provide a relaxing and healing feeling to the child or teenager. Younger children need the presence of their parents in order to undergo massage therapy, while older children, including adolescents may prefer to be alone with the massage therapist. These children are given the opportunity to direct therapists, albeit by guidance and support from their parents. The child's feelings must be respected and followed.

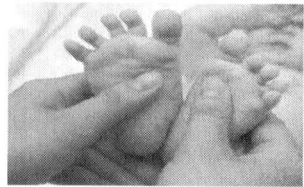 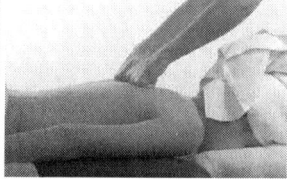

Figure 13: Massage therapy for a baby (A) and a teenager (B).

Acupuncture:

This is a traditional Chinese methodology that involves use of fine, thin needles that are introduced into acupuncture points on the skin to elicit a given feeling. This ancient therapy can be used to relieve symptoms of anxiety, especially in teenagers. It is believed that the manipulation of these needles produces a positive flow of energy within the body that relieves anxiety.

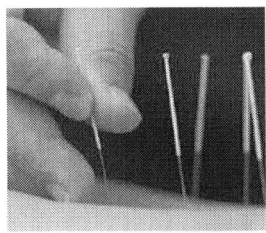 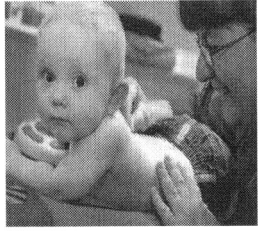

Figure 14: A holistic therapist performing acupuncture.

Healing Energy:

Children have a lot of energy, both positive and negative, and manipulating either of them tremendously affects how a child behaves and handles stress. To treat children with anxiety, the holistic therapist must ensure that he or she balances both the negative energies with positive ones. Of the many forms of healing energy modalities available, two of the most common are Polarity and Reiki. The healers are well acquainted with energy patterns and use techniques such as creative visualization and pure intention to direct the flow of energy. While in session, the therapist places his hands above the children, or on them to allow free energy to flow, and heal the anxious child. The children get accustomed to their new energy pattern and can then practice this technique whenever they experience their fears and worries.

Hypnotherapy:

This type of therapy is based on the concept of hypnosis (sleep of the nervous system). Hypnotized patients show susceptibility to suggestions, and this can be used to enforce behavior change in an anxious child or a teenager. It uses active imagination, positive attitude, expectations and motivational strategies to give the child a way out of his or her stressful situations. This module of therapy is very effective if used with cognitive-behavioral change (CBT) to treat anxiety in children and teenagers.

Playing and Exercising:

It has been established that children find peace and pleasure when they play with their peers. When play and exercise are integrated in the healing sessions, anxious children are able to build healthy relationships, helping them to forget their traumatic experiences and fears, as well as establishing feelings of personal safety.

Figure 15: Parents playing and exercising with their children.

Creative Visualization:

to explore. This type of therapy involves establishing positive thoughts and images in the mind to effect healing. Most anxious children or teenagers recognize the sources of their anxiety as their negative thoughts or unusual images they conceive in their minds. These are introduced at therapy sessions where the correct thoughts and right images are introduced, and the child can use these in between the sessions to bring them peace and emotional healing.

Music:

It has long been known that music enhances memory and soothes the mind, creating a positive energy that helps with emotional healing. Music works to influence the subconscious mind, helping the child forget his or her worries during the therapy sessions. They can then practice this with parents at home every time they feel like they are "losing it."

Nutrition:

Although quite controversial, the diet one has seems to have some influence on their emotional, mental and physical status. Some of the substances parts of the brain uses to communicate with each other (neurotransmitters) are synthesized from certain food types taken. An excess or deficiency of these substances can lead to behavior patterns similar to those manifested by anxious children and teenagers. A balanced diet containing enough proteins helps the body in the manufacture of stimulatory substances such as serotonin, dopamine, epinephrine and norepinephrine. Food should also be taken regularly and timely, as disorganized eating habits may lead to poor appetite and therefore anxiety.

Emotional Expression:

In order for us to grow emotionally into healthy adults our emotions should be expressed freely. Childhood and teenage anxiety usually is the result of repressed emotions, so it is important to encourage children and teenagers to express their feelings freely and learn to control them. In addition, these feelings should be accepted, and validated because punishing or opposing them could also make the anxiety worse. If your family is not a family where emotional expression is a common practice, professional help may be needed to get this process started.

Parents can help children become more aware of their feelings and emotions. If something is gently bothering them, or a stressful situation is gradually about to take place, you can detect the predictable event to likely occur and remove them from it. For example, Johnny decided to play with Mark one day instead of your child. As a parent you can detect that this event could slowly upset and cause your child to have anxious feelings. You can teach them the ability to detect stressful situations and remove themselves from circumstances that hurt them. The more they are able to better understand their own feelings and emotions, the more likely they are to keep them in check.

Teach them how to control their emotions and stay relaxed. Deep breathing techniques can often come in handy at this stage. It is important not to reach the boiling point, and try to calm the body and mind. Try to bring the body temperature back to normal in order to control your anxiety. This will eventually help in regulating your state of anxiety arousal. Help develop small changes in your child's thinking patterns. This way they can manage emotions better and understand reality clearly. Teach them how to use empathy to understand how other people might deal with this problem, or how it would feel like to walk in their shoes.

You can play games with them that can raise their emotional awareness and be better able to identify people's emotions and feelings. The next time you take your child driving around in the car, you can play a game with them and ask them to generally recognize how that person walking outside is feeling. The child can use his or her body language, facial expressions, and style of behavior to access what mood they are in. This will help improve the child's ability to recognize emotions and feelings in other people too.

You can even use them in an example; put a couple of different CD's on and ask the child to listen to each of the songs. While they are listening to the different tone, voices and intensity of song ask them to describe what they feel during the different songs. Does the song make them feel like getting up and dancing, feeling sad or maybe makes them happy? This will help get them more in touch with their feelings and emotions.

Other Calming Exercises for Children

When it comes to relaxation exercises, the key is to practice them while you're **not** anxious. Conscious relaxation is a muscle that needs to be strengthened. Most of us don't give it a second thought until we're feeling overwhelmed with anxiety. Work with your child on relaxation anytime a small window of time opens up. Even 1-2 minutes is enough. That's the beauty of it.

Deep breathing: Even a toddler can do this. It's easy for them to pick up immediately, if you breathe with them. Teach children the ability to breathe using the lower parts of their lungs. Deep breathing has been labeled as the secret solution to some of the most common mood swings. Explain to your children how deep breathing can often calm the mind and body. Deep breathing can help calm the amygdala which causes the responses of our stress hormones. You can explain to your child that the amygdala is like the old security watch dog who stands at the front of the gate. Whenever the amygdala perceives threatening behavior, it starts alerting and sending signals and stress hormones all throughout our body.

The art of mindful breathing would allow them to calm the amygdala, which is in some cases is overly sensitive to the external surroundings around us. Teach your children to incorporate five minutes of deep breathing into their lives every day. Deep breathing also helps by releasing good hormones such as dopamine and serotonin.

Deep breathing allows us to strengthen our self-reflective abilities, self-awareness, and increase emotional control, which can result in better control of our anxiety. Tell them to place their hand on their bellies as they are taking in deep breaths, and exhale out slowly. Feel the diaphragm fill with air as they inhale.

Playing games that make them become aware of their pulse rate and breathing patterns are also very helpful. Tell your child to sit down in a quiet room and place their two fingers on their wrists, locating their pulse, and gently hold their fingers there. Then tell them to count the number of the pulse rate that occurs in one minute.

After they have counted the total number of times for the pulse rate, tell them to go run outside for 3-4 minutes. They can do jumping jacks, run in the backyard or any other kind of small physical activity. When they are done, tell them to return to their quiet corner and place their fingers over their wrist again, and count the number of the pulse rate that occurs for one minute.

Showing them the difference in the changes of the pulse rates allows them to understand the changes in their body and heart rate. They can gradually use this technique to figure out if they are angry or not. Being in touch with their pulse rate, and understanding their pulse rate can be important for children to monitor their angry behavior. Teach them what normal expected pulse rates are, and what extreme pulse rates can be.

• **Progressive Muscle Relaxation**: This exercise helps define tension and relaxation. Systematically go through the body, clenching and releasing muscle groups. Smaller children will need a demonstration. It may be as simple as, "Make your hands into fists and squeeze. Now make your hands sleep." Older kids can probably lie down, close their eyes and follow along with verbal cues, taking them through the different parts of the body.

• **Stretching:** Good old fashioned stretching. Yoga is great, relax! Turn on your computer's visualizer and watch the dynamic abstract shapes. Here are some great stretching sites to explore:

http://www.bing.com/images/search?q=stretching+exercises&qpvt=stretching+exercises&FORM=IGRE

http://www.mayoclinic.com/health/stretching/SM00043

http://www.ehow.com/sports/fitness/stretching/

Physical exercises for children

Anxious children can also have problems in sensory processing. They react without control to some sensory stimuli. Most of the time, they try to maintain their balance by keeping their head up straight in a tense way instead of using the support and the solidity of the ground. As a result anxious children do not like to be moved and very often they move very little themselves. Although it is important that they will have more physical exercise and start to enjoy this, it is necessary for them to experience more body awareness and start to use the ground for support. Finding support on the ground or on their parents' lap will relax them and their fear will diminish.

The following activities and games may be suitable:

- Domestic activities
- Provide enough physical exercise
- The use of weights
- The use of vibrating material
- Sitting on a ball or ball cushion
- Sitting on a ball and moving to music
- Sitting on a ball while watching television
- Exercise pressure with a ball
- Lying on top of different materials
- Swaddling or wrapping up in a blanket
- Rolling, walking on your knees or on all fours over different materials
- Skating on rugs
- Touching and moving on your lap
- Something to feel
- Playing with shaving cream
- Playing with rice
- Playing with chestnuts
- Rubbing in body lotion

- Massage with different materials
- The use of the foot massage bath
- Blowing bubbles

Exercise will vary depending on the age of child! The key to these methods are taking the child's mind on a journey that will make them forget about the problems at hand, this will give you time to talk as well.

Indications for Holistic Therapy

Not every anxious child or teenager can benefit from these holistic approaches for treatment of anxiety. One important thing to remember is that all of these treatments are subject to a consultation with an accredited holistic healthcare provider, and a psychiatrist or psychologist. Here are the indications for holistic therapy:

- Mild to moderate anxiety in older children and adolescents, as some of these treatments cannot be practiced with very young children.

- If treatment with home remedies fail to produce any noticeable improvement after protracted periods of practice.

- If holistic therapy is safer than medications in moderate to severe anxiety, due to side effects of such drugs.

- On the advice of a pediatric psychiatrist or psychologist handling the anxious patient.

- The child or teenager under treatment should be able to understand what is being done and can participate, because these methods deal with the individual as a person.

- If anxiety occurs in conjunction with depression, a holistic approach can be used to treat both if the professionals agree.

Contraindications of Holistic Therapy

- Patients with very severe life-disabling forms of anxiety cannot benefit from the holistic therapy modalities.

- Children and teenagers with acute forms of anxiety, such as panic attacks may need medications instead of holistic approaches. This is because holistic therapy needs time to implement and produce a positive effect.

- Lack of response for protracted periods of time following holistic therapy disqualifies further use.

- Very young children who cannot comprehend and practice the holistic therapy methods may not respond to treatment.

Cognitive-Behavioral Therapy

Referred to as CBT, cognitive-behavioral therapy involves organizing talk sessions between the therapist and the child. This typically involves talk sessions lasting about twelve weeks, during which the therapist teaches the child techniques and skills that he or she can use to relieve the symptoms of anxiety.

The point of focus in CBT is replacing the negative, pessimistic thoughts characteristic of anxiety with positive, optimistic ones. It also helps the children to recognize what is real from what is not. These are learned and incorporated as homework that the child has to do and therefore practices them in the process. Once learned, the techniques can help the child to deal with anxiety even in the future. In addition to sessions with the child, the therapist also ensures that the child carries on normally with school work and home. It is also important that other family members also learn to support the anxious child, and so should receive training from the therapist.

In CBT, life is segmented into five areas that influence the sense of well-being, the emotions and behavior. These are situation, thoughts, emotions, physical feelings and responses (actions). A situation represents the problem, the difficulty, or the presenting event for which a reaction is expected. This event is then followed by a thought, which if negative, produces the disturbed emotions, the physical response of anxiety, and the abnormal responses seen in these children. CBT aims to change the negative thoughts, thereby changing the entire response.

CBT is a relatively new modality for the treatment of anxiety and depression, and therefore much research has not been done to authoritatively measure its effectiveness. However testimonials from those who have used it successfully have helped come up with some advantages and disadvantages that are worthwhile to know.

Advantages of CBT

- Cognitive-behavioral therapy is effective in many cases of anxiety co-occurring with depression.

- It is often as effective as anxiolytics (drugs for treating anxiety), and antidepressants in the treatment of anxiety and depression respectively.

- CBT has virtually no side effects, and therefore is safer as compared to the use of anxiolytics and antidepressants.

- It is considered the best psychological treatment option for moderate and severe forms of anxiety and depression.

- The child or teenager is able to understand themselves better, in terms of why some behaviors occur and how to best handle them naturally.

- CBT is short term, cost effective and issue based, and therefore saves time and money for both the therapist and the client.

Disadvantages of CBT

- This form of therapy requires very high levels of commitment not easy to achieve for most individuals, especially children and teenagers. This could lead to many failed experiences.

- CBT tends to work well with those with mild to moderate mental conditions. Some children and teenagers with complex disorders may not be able to learn, commit and involve themselves in the treatment process.

- Another possible disadvantage given by those opposing the use of CBT is that it is issue-based, and therefore its spectrum is not large enough to address and treat the underlying mental disorder that manifests with anxiety.

Medical Treatment of Childhood and Teenage Anxiety

For many years before the development of CBT, the mainstay of anxiety treatment has been the use of medications. These are referred to as anxiolytics. Because anxiety is usually, but not always present in combination with depression, antidepressants are also used. Several classes of drugs are available for this purpose as will be discussed below. However, before delving into discussion of specific drugs, there are some interesting facts.

Facts about Anxiety Medications

• Like other drugs, anxiolytics and antidepressants have unwanted side-effects which can exacerbate the problem, or cause newer medical conditions that warrant discontinuation.

• Some of the side-effects may need to be treated too, making this modality of treatment even more expensive.

• Use of medications alone may not be as effective as a combination therapy with CBT, and therefore an anxious child or teenager will have to attend the therapy session, and also take medication.

- Some of these drugs are more dangerous for children and teenagers than adults, therefore a parent must always consult his or her doctor before embarking on this form of treatment.

- Very severe, life threatening forms of anxiety and depression have to be treated with medications to remove the root cause of the problem. These severe cases do not respond to other modalities of therapy, and can cause life altering problems if left untreated.

- Dependencies as well as tolerance are two important effects that can result from the use of these medications, as will discussed below. They may have serious impact on a child's or teenager's development.

Drugs Treating Childhood and Teenage Anxiety

Although over-the-counter medications exist for anxiety, self-medication is generally not recommended for children and adolescents. Moreover, one of the worst results of anxiety disorders is suicide tendencies, which can be caused by an overdose of such medications. Most medication treatments are however prescription drugs approved by the drug agencies.

Classification of Anti-Anxiety Drugs

This classification is based on the mechanism of action of the drugs for better understanding. Each of the categories has specific indications, contraindications and side effect profiles.

Antidepressants

Anti-depressants are drugs that act in the brain as stimulants. Authorities believe that anxiety and depression develop from imbalances in various amino acids that act as mediators and neurotransmitters in the brain (this is called amine theory of depression). These substances include dopamine, nor epinephrine, epinephrine and serotonin. Of the antidepressants, selective serotonin inhibitors (SSRIs) are the most commonly used because of their safety profile and efficacy.

SSRIs

How Do They Work?

Serotonin is a neurotransmitter (a substance found in the brain cells that help in communication between different parts of the brain) with stimulatory effects. Anxiety and depression result from lack of brain stimulation because of reduced levels of stimulatory amino acids. After the release of serotonin from the brain cells, it is taken up by scavenger cells within the vicinity of the responding cell. This terminates its effects of stimulating the brain. SSRIs prevent reuptake of serotonin, allowing it a longer time to sojourn in the vicinity of the responding cell, leading to longer stimulatory action. The prototype and the most commonly used of SSRIs is Fluoxetine (Prozac) and will be discussed in detail below. Others in this class are Sertraline (Zoloft), Paroxetine (Paxil), Fluvoxamine (Luvox), Citalopram (Celexa), and Escitalopram (Lexapro).

Fluoxetine (Prozac): this is the longest serving of the SSRIs that has been successfully used to treat anxiety and depression in children and adolescents for years. It is used in children and adolescents aged between eight and eighteen years.

Indications

Not everyone with anxiety disorders benefits from this medicine. In children and teenagers, the following conditions respond well to fluoxetine;

- Major depression in children aged eight years to eighteen years

- Obsessive compulsive disorder (OCD) in children aged seven years to eighteen years

Efficacy and Dosage

This drug is effective, but the effects are often not seen until after four weeks of administration. Lower weight children (weight smaller than that of children of similar age) require lower starting doses (10 mg/day) gradually increased with therapy. The maximum dosage for children and adolescents with major depression is 20 mg/day. The therapy is short term, lasting eight to nine weeks. The dosages are higher for patients with obsessive compulsive disorder, ranging from 10 to 60 mg/day.

Side Effects

SSRIs are the safest of the antidepressants. This is due to their relative selectivity in the brain, as compared to other nonselective drugs in this class. Any unwanted side-effects may warrant discontinuation of treatment, or change to another antidepressant. When very severe, the side-effects themselves may need medical treatment. The side effects can be grouped as common, rare and serious.

Common Side Effects

- Generalized headache, relieved by painkillers.

- Gastrointestinal disturbances- The child complains of nausea, vomiting and diarrhea or constipation. These are quite nonspecific and can be overlooked.

- The child experiences jitters/tremor that mimics Parkinson's Disease that may make them uncomfortable. This is sometimes referred to as restless leg syndrome.

- Disturbance in falling and staying asleep (insomnia). In addition these children experience somnolence, vivid dreams as well as nightmares. This may interfere with the children's academic performance, as they tend to fall asleep while in class.

- The drug can interact with other antidepressant drugs in the class, except Sertraline (Zoloft) interfering with plasma levels and therefore their actions.

- In adolescents and late teenagers, it may cause sexual dysfunction manifesting as delayed ejaculation or orgasm impairment.

- Weight gain is another side effect that is associated with fluoxetine use. Parents may need to keep a watchful eye on these children, as they may be prone to develop obesity due to changes in appetite.

- Tolerance to the drug. This means reduction in efficacy of the drug with continued use, which warrants upping the dose or changing medications.

Rare Side Effects

These side effects occur in only a small number of children and teenagers receiving fluoxetine. They include agitation, irritability and high impulsivity. If a child or a teenager develops these side effects, then it is more likely that they are acquiring a bipolar disorder. This is especially true if the child has suffered from mania or hypomania before, or there is an established family history of bipolar disorder.

Serious Life-Threatening Side Effects

These side effects need to be reported immediately when they are identified in a child or a teenager. In this case discontinuation is imminent as further therapy may lead to death. Parents of children and adolescents should be very aware in order to identify the manifestations of these symptoms, and seek medical attention from their doctor or qualified clinician. The side effects include:

- Suicidal thoughts and tendencies. These children always think of dying as the only solution to their problems, and a certain percentage end up making attempts which may actually succeed. It occurs in children, adolescents and young adults aged between eighteen and twenty four years.

- Sudden discontinuation of the drug, either due to side effects or non compliance, may cause new or worsening anxiety as well as depression in children and teens under medication.

- Severe agitation, restlessness, anger, and violence that is usually uncontrollable.

- Episodes of severe panic attacks characterized by accelerated heart beats and breathing problems.

- Bizarre behavior and mood changes interfering with social life.

- Some children develop symptoms of mania characterized by very fast speech, as if under pressure, racing thoughts, and the propensity to take risks regardless of the outcome.

Antihistamines

Histamine is also another neurotransmitter found in the brain and other parts of the body, including blood cells and the gastrointestinal system. In the brain, histamine acts as a stimulator of brain activity, and therefore acts similarly to serotonin, but not as selective because of the presence of histamine receptors in other organs. Although they have been in use for some time for the treatment of anxiety, official controlled studies have not been done to support their use. The antihistamines in use for treatment of pediatric anxiety are Diphenhydramine (Benadryl), and Hydroxyzine (Vistaril, Atarax).

Indications of Antihistamines

Of the two drugs the most commonly used for treatment of anxiety is hydroxyzine (Vistaril, Atarax), and it is available as a prescription drug. Diphenhydramine, on the other hand, is not officially used for anxiety disorders, but its side effect of sedation is what is used to calm children with anxiety, and to help them sleep. Hydroxyzine is used to treat generalized anxiety disorder and obsessive compulsive disorder (OCD) in children and teenagers.

Side Effects

Most of these reactions are written on the manufactures label, and so parents can read them before deciding whether or not to go for such medication for their children.

• Dizziness, lack of coordination and very deep sleep, which may interfere with the child's daily activities.

• Gastrointestinal disturbances are also common, and include: nausea and vomiting, constipation, diarrhea and discomfort.

• Overdose may lead to hallucinations and confusion in children and adolescents using hydroxyzine for anxiety.

• Somnolence occurring with vivid dreams and nightmares has been recorded in patients using this medicine.

Benefits of Using Hydroxyzine

The drug does not exhibit any properties attributable to dependence or withdrawal. In addition, hydroxyzine • has a mild sedative and hypnotic effect, which make it safer than other anti-anxiety drugs which have more profound effects. This drug produces a calming effect without interfering with attention, concentration, or memory.

Beta-Blockers

The human body works by messenger system. This means that for bodily functions to be coordinated, information must be sent from one part of the body to another. In this complex system, there are substances that act as messengers from one organ, or part of the body, to another in order to produce a given response. One of the messengers is a substance called _adrenaline hormone_. It is released in response to anxiety, causing some of the symptoms of anxiety, such as shaking, tremors, sweating, racing heart beats, and rapid breathing. This hormone produces its effects when it attaches to its receptors (known as Beta-adrenergic receptors). Beta-blockers are drugs that attach to these receptors, blocking the effects of the hormone. Beta-blockers therefore do not treat anxiety, but its manifesting symptoms.

The main use of Beta-blockers is in the treatment of hypertension, hyperactive thyroid disorders and chest pain due to heart disease (angina pectoris), however, they are used off-label to treat anxiety in children and teenagers. The ones commonly used in childhood anxiety are propranolol (Inderal) and atenolol (Tenormin). Other beta-blockers include acebutolol, bisoprolol, carvedilol, celiprolol, esmolol, labetalol, metoprolol, nadolol, nebivolol, oxprenolol, pindolol, sotalol and timolol.

Indications of Beta-Blockers

Beta-blockers have no effect on the emotional status and cannot be used for long-term therapy of anxiety. However, they are very effective in the treatment of symptoms associated with anxious situations. This means that they can be used in panic attacks and phobias such as performance anxiety, and social phobias. They can be taken by children or teenagers who have anticipatory anxiety, such as being called upon to give a speech in front of classmates or any kind of audiences.

Side Effects of Beta-Blockers

The side effects of Beta-blockers are rare if appropriate dosage for children and teenagers is used. The dosage depends on the patient's age, and a doctor should be sought to make the decision whether to medicate an anxious child with beta-blockers. The possible side effects include:

• Bradycardia (very slow heart rate) may occur in some children treated with beta-blockers. This may manifest as dizziness, syncope (fainting) and profound weakness. This side-effect needs treatment, because it can lead to death due to heart failure if not corrected.

• Cold extremities (hands and feet) results from narrowing of the small blood vessels supplying the peripheral structures.

• Sleeping disorders in some patients, characterized by vivid dreams and nightmares.

• For sexually active teenagers, beta-blockers may cause impotence and erectile dysfunction because of blunted response due to beta-adrenergic receptor blockade.

• In children with type I diabetes mellitus, beta-blockers may mask the manifestations of low blood sugar levels (hypoglycemia) which usually present with palpitations (awareness of heartbeats) and fine tremors (shaking).

• Light-headedness, nausea and sometimes vomiting have also been reported in children and teenagers receiving beta-blockers.

Contraindications of Beta-Blockers

- As discussed above, diabetic patients should not receive beta blockers, because warning signs of poorly controlled sugar levels are blunted. This can lead to the development of life-threatening hypoglycemia, or hyperglycemia and ketonemia (manifesting as diabetic ketoacidosis).

- Beta-blockers are also contraindicated in asthmatic children. This is because asthma is an airway narrowing disorder, an affect produced by beta-blockade. This synergism can produce worsening or even a life threatening asthmatic attack.

- These drugs should also not be used in children with anxiety who also suffer from any heart disease. This is because beta-blockade increases stress on the heart's performance, and therefore their use may cause the heat to fail due to decompensation.

Benzodiazepines

These are the most widely used anti-anxiety drugs. They are effective tranquilizers (freeing from stress and emotions), and anxiety relievers. They have a very calming effect, which has made them very popular for use in the treatment of anxiety in children and adolescents, as well as adults. As will be discussed later, the major problem limiting the use of benzodiazepines in children is tolerance and withdrawal symptoms.

How Do Benzodiazepines Work?

In simple terms, benzodiazepines work by slowing the activity of the brain and the spinal cord (central nervous system). They produce this by potentiating the effects of specific receptors in the brain known as Gamma-amino butyric Acid (GABA) receptors. These receptors deliver inhibitory impulses to brain activity therefore slowing it. This produces a calming effect, and therefore relieving anxiety. At the same time, benzodiazepines cause sedation which can help anxious children with their sleeping disorders.

Indications of Benzodiazepines

In children with anxiety disorders, these drugs are effective in the treatment of acute panic attacks, phobic disorders, generalized anxiety disorder, attention deficit syndrome, disinhibition and obsessive compulsive disorder. They have rapid onset of action, producing their effects in as short as four hours. These drugs should not be used alone, as this increases the risk of side effects, tolerance and more severe withdrawal symptoms. The medication therapy is more likely to be shortened if psychotherapy is used alongside the benzodiazepines.

Examples of Benzodiazepines used in Children and Teenagers

The best known and the most popularly used benzodiazepine is diazepam (Valium). This is because it is available in generic forms, which are not only cheaper, but are also as effective as the original. In addition, most general practitioners as well as pediatricians have wide experience with this drug. Diazepam has a longer duration of action, which makes dosing infrequent and therefore easing compliance.

The other benzodiazepine which can be used in children and teenagers is lorazepam (Ativan). The advantage of using this drug lies in its short action, which can be used for children with episodes of disinhibition. It is not used in generalized anxiety disorder because of the frequency of dosing, which may reduce compliance. Other benzodiazepines that can be used to treat anxiety in children include clonazepam and alprazolam, but they have limiting disadvantages.

Side Effects of Benzodiazepines

Benzodiazepines are quite safe to be used in children and teenagers, but the use may be limited by the potential development of side effects. When severe, these side effects may warrant discontinuation of the medication. The longer a child or a teenager is exposed to these drugs, the more likelihood that they will develop the side effects. In addition to the side effects, these drugs are addictive, and therefore can easily be abused by teenagers. The most common limiting problems with benzodiazepines are tolerance and withdrawal. These will be discussed later.

Rare Side Effects Occurring in less than 10% of the Children on Benzodiazepines

- Somnolence: This is among the most common side effects of these drugs. It is due to the action of the drug in the brain. When the activity of the brain is slowed, the child may feel so sleepy and drowsy that they cannot be attentive. This may interfere with their academics and lead to failure.

• Lack of coordination: Anxious children treated with benzodiazepines may not be able to coordinate their body movements. This may interfere with writing and performing skilled actions using their hands. This could lead to serious consequences in their social and intellectual developments.

•: This is an abnormal walking gait seen in children and teenagers treated with benzodiazepines. It is the result of its effects on certain brain centers concerned with balance and gait. When this is noticed, the child experiencing this reaction should be closely watched, because they are prone to accidents. Seek immediate advice from a doctor.

• Diarrhea: Some children may also suffer from diarrhea, which can cause mal-absorption and interfere with the child's growth. This is due to the loss of important nutrients from the gastrointestinal tract.

Common Side Effects

• **Hypotension**: Children and teenagers on management for anxiety for a long time with benzodiazepines may suffer from very low blood pressure. The parent or caretaker of the child will notice reduced activity, and frequent squatting or kneeling to avoid falling. They must also be followed closely to avoid injuries. If not corrected, hypotension can lead to brain and heart damage. Seek medical attention for this problem!

• **Unexplained fatigue**: Extreme weakness is associated with benzodiazepine use. These children complain of extreme tiredness, even without performing any activity. This can limit their playing, studying and performing simple tasks. Medical advice is required here.

• **Respiratory problems**: This is one of the most dangerous side effects, because it can cause respiratory depression, manifesting as chest tightness and difficulty in breathing. This may limit activities that need exertion, such as playing with peers or exercising. Seek medical attention for this problem!

• **Muscle weakness**: This may make playing and even walking very difficult. If this is recognized, the parent or caretaker needs to take appropriate actions to ensure this is addressed.

Serious Side Effects

• **Neutropenia**: This is a reduction (below normal) of the total number of white blood cells called neutrophils responsible for protecting the body against infections. Children and teenagers receiving benzodiazepines are prone to develop neutropenia, a condition that can predispose them to infections.

• **Local effects at the injection site**: These include thrombophlebitis (inflammation of veins at the site of benzodiazepine injection), pain and swelling of the site of injection, carpal tunnel syndrome (painful swelling if the wrist joint due to compression of a nerve within a tunnel formed by carpal bones), and tissue necrosis (death of tissues at the site of injection). These can cause serous discomfort and deformities at the local level. This is an issue only for those who receive their medication via injection.

- **Phlebitis with rapid intravenous infusion of benzodiazepines.** Thus this drug should be administered by slow infusion.

Benzodiazepine Tolerance, Dependence and Withdrawal Syndrome

Tolerance means that with protracted use of these drugs, a larger dose is needed to produce the desired therapeutic effect. As this occurs, the potential for side effects become more severe, because of the increased dosage. Tolerance develops from the desensitization of the gamma amino butyric acid receptors, which are the mediators of benzodiazepine actions. The initial manifestation of tolerance is a failure of the drugs to relieve anxiety at the prescribed dosage, and therefore the child needs a higher dose to get the beneficial effects of the drugs.

When management of anxiety with benzodiazepines is suddenly stopped, the outcome can either be a rebound or withdrawal syndrome. These are referred to as dependence related responses. Rebound means that the initial complaint for which treatment was sought returns after what was considered a successful treatment. If this is not the case, the child or teenager develops a constellation of new complaints known as the withdrawal syndrome. The manifestations of withdrawal syndrome are sometimes very severe and may warrant additional treatment.

The symptoms of withdrawal syndrome include insomnia (difficulty in initiating and staying asleep), stomach disturbances, tremors, extreme fearfulness, muscle spasms (involuntary contraction of muscles) and agitation. Other less common manifestations include drenching sweat, easy irritability, and high sensitivity to external stimuli, depersonalization, depression, suicidal tendencies, seizures, psychosis and delirium. These symptoms are more severe with very rapid or very abrupt discontinuation of benzodiazepine therapy. Even with gradual discontinuation, some degree of withdrawal syndrome occurs, but it is mild and protracted in the slow course. These symptoms lessen in severity with time and eventually disappear altogether.

Treatment of Withdrawal Syndrome Symptoms

The use of benzodiazepines alone can cause severe withdrawal symptoms. This is why doctors recommend the use of psychotherapy in conjunction with benzodiazepines to manage children and teenagers with withdrawal syndrome. Withdrawal symptoms are common with short-acting benzodiazepines, and therefore one of the management strategies is to replace them with longer-acting benzodiazepines such as diazepam.

Contraindications and Drug Interactions

In an attempt to manage the withdrawal symptoms of benzodiazepines in children and teenagers receiving these medications, inexperienced doctors may prescribe other classes of drugs. These drugs can adversely interact with benzodiazepines to cause new symptoms, or worsen the existing withdrawal symptoms. The following reactions occur:

- **Alcohol-** The use of this is rare in children, but may occur in late teenage years. This is because alcohol is cross tolerant with benzodiazepines and therefore more toxic.

- **Non-benzodiazepines whose actions are also mediated by GABA** should not be used with benzodiazepines, or during withdrawal symptoms, because of cross-tolerance and dependence.

- **Some antibiotics-** If a child or a teenager gets a bacterial infection while on management for withdrawal symptoms, care should be taken to avoid fluoroquinolones. This is because they dislodge benzodiazepines from the GABA receptors, reducing their functions and worsening the side effects.

- **Antipsychotic drugs-** Anxious children and teenagers who also suffer from psychosis as a result of benzodiazepine use should not be managed with antipsychotic drugs. This is because these drugs depress the central nervous system activity, causing seizures and worsening withdrawal symptoms.

Other Anti-Anxiety Medications

A wide range of other available drugs are considered to have some anxiolytic activities, although they have not officially been approved for the treatment of anxiety in children and teenagers. Among the most promising is buspirone. This drug is highly effective in binding to serotonin receptors and mediates its effect in a similar fashion to the selective serotonin receptor inhibitors (SSRIs).

Buspirone (BuSpar)

Indications

BuSpar is used unofficially in the treatment of anxiety disorders in children and teenagers. Though it has shown some success in the treatment of anxiety, the drug is yet to be approved for use, though it is available in both original and generic forms. It has been used in the treatment of the following anxiety disorders; generalized anxiety disorder, panic attacks, obsessive compulsive disorder and depression in children and teenagers with generalized anxiety disorder. Buspirone can be used for acute relief of anxiety or long-term management of anxiety disorders.

Advantages

This drug is available as Buspirone hydrochloride. Although its efficacy has not been approved for treatment of childhood and teenage anxiety, it has numerous advantages that warrant its usage. First, this drug does not cross-react with benzodiazepines, making it safe to use after the discontinuation of benzodiazepines. Second, there is very low risk for tolerance and dependence. This allows for prolonged use without having to worry about development of withdrawal symptoms. Third, unlike the other drugs used to treat anxiety in children and teenagers, buspirone does not cause sedation, making it safe for school-going children and teenagers. Finally, buspirone is quite selective for serotonin receptors, which minimize the spectrum of its side effects.

__Disadvantages and Side-Effects of Buspirone__

The most prominent disadvantage associated with buspirone use is that it takes up to four weeks to achieve its optimal efficacy or effectiveness, and so cannot be used for acute(immediate) anxiety disorders. The common side effects of buspirone include:

- Dizziness
- Lightheadedness
- Nausea, sometimes with vomiting
- Headache
- Nervousness
- Euphoria
- Insomnia

Other rare side effects associated with buspirone use are:

- Disturbances in gait (unsteadiness)
- Shaking, tremors and rigors
- Unexplained excitement
- Easy irritability and hostility
- Diarrhea
- Skin rashes
- Muscle weaknesses

Hints for Parents and Caretakers

There are several approaches that can be used by parents and other family members to help children and teenagers deal with anxiety. These revolve around offering home support and reassurance to the child. They are discussed below:

Establishing predictable routines

Maintaining a structural way of doing things in the home reduces anxiety in children. This works because the children can always predict the outcome of these routines, thereby solving the "uncertainty characteristic" of anxiety. Research has shown than children at risk of anxiety definitely develop this disorder if they have to cope with disorganized, unpredictable family lifestyles.

Parents or caretakers should establish regular bedtimes, mealtimes, and school times. A quieting style, such as reciting or narrating bedtime stories, and talking and reading with the children help them to relax until sleep takes over. This should be done in a regular, structured and predictable manner. Outline restrictions for the child, and help them understand the consequences of operating outside of these restrictions.

Help children characterize their feelings

Children who get anxious often have feelings that they harbor inside, because they do not know how to express them. Help children identify and express their feelings by showing them how to react visually and audibly in different situations. For example, show feelings using facial expressions, verbal expressions and body movements. <u>Children must be convinced that expressing their feelings is the only way that others can understand them.</u> They will also recognize that they feel better when they express their feelings appropriately.

Communication About Feelings

One of the best ways to deal with anxiety is talking about the fears and worries. For children, this is not easy and therefore parents must create opportunities to talk about their feelings. Children cannot adequately communicate their feelings as adults would do, but with encouragement and carefully observing their behaviors and listening to words uttered by them, parents can always tell that a child is anxious. Be that as it may, unacceptable feelings should not be rebuked directly as this would weaken the child's feelings even further. They would feel that they disappointed you, and are being disapproved and unaccepted, which are other sources of anxiety.

Showing concern and respect for the child's feelings and fears

Children may be young and naïve, but they do have feelings of their own. It is disastrous to discredit or ignore these feelings, because as far as they are concerned, the feelings are true. It doesn't help if you tell a child not to be afraid. It actually might even make the anxiety worse. The parents or caretakers should instead show concern and respect for their child's fears, and make the child feel that the parents are there to help them deal with fears and overcome the worries.

Reassurance And Comforting Tactics

Anxious children benefit very much from verbal reassurances and soothing and comforting actions. Children need to be cuddled, massaged, held close, and rocked, in addition to being sung to, showed love and told soothing and comforting stories.

Children with anxiety disorders are special. They may need soothing tactics that seem too childlike for their age, as far as the parent or caretaker is concerned. These children may react better to reassuring and comforting than the 'appropriate' strategies.

Behavior Modeling

The hallmark of anxiety is fear and panic, therefore adopting brave behavior is a key component in helping children deal with this condition. Just like everyone else, children are often afraid of situations that they are not familiar with, and therefore look to others around them for guidance on how to respond. Children skillfully and subconsciously watch parents and older siblings for clues on the appropriate response to different situations, including those they fear.

Anything short of bravery spells doom to the child, because he does not have the confidence to respond bravely. Parents who overprotect their children, or those who are anxious themselves can pass on this trait to their children promoting anxiety. A parent who is anxious ought to handle their anxiety appropriately while in the presence of their children, as this goes a long way in helping these children to contain their own anxious moments. It wouldn't hurt for a few parents to be seeking professional help for their anxiety, and their children might realize that it is okay to get help.

Promote And Reward Bravery

Traditionally it is known that rewarding good behavior or any other achievements for that matter reinforces such behavior or performance. This is a conditioning system that has been scientifically proven, and can be employed to help anxious children. Telling children to face their fears is counter-productive, but gradual introduction and guidance on how to respond bravely helps the children to learn one step at a time, which is more comfortable to them.

Conclusion

Anxiety in preteens and teens is a common problem in many, if not all societies and cultures. It is responsible for health problems, and personality problems, as well as relationship and success problems. Teenage alcoholism, drug addiction, suicide attempts and some crimes may result from unresolved anxiety disorders developed in early childhood. However, if this anxiety is recognized early by parents, and professionals, by looking for the telltale signs and symptoms discussed above, even children born to families with such mental disorders can live normal, healthy lives.

It is clear that parents and caretakers play a very important role in the social as well as emotional development of a child. The way that children can handle their fears and worries, depends on how these important people deal with their own fears and worries. Therefore, parents and caretakers ought to exude optimal confidence when faced with scary situations, so that their children can emulate this behavior. Although that doesn't mean that it is not okay to have "normal" fear of certain things. Parents ought to also help children learn that they can feel safe, even when they are nervous or anxious. If a child knows that a parent is helping him/her to feel safe, then it is easier for the child to reframe the situation and start feeling safe, instead of scared and anxious.

Holistic therapy, behavior manipulation, cognitive-behavioral therapy, and medications are the management modalities used in treating anxiety in teens and preteens. They work more effectively when used in combination. To crown it all, the immediate family of the child has the huge responsibility to ensure that the anxious children find comfort, acceptance, and relief from anxiety.

Links

Article: Childhood Anxiety Disorders
http://www.adaa.org/living-with-anxiety/children/childhood-anxiety-disorders

Article: The Anxious Child
http://www.aacap.org/cs/root/facts_for_families/the_anxious_child

Article: Anxiety in Children—How Parents Can Help.
http://www.kathyeugster.com/articles/article004.htm

Article: Generalized Anxiety Disorder
http://www.mayoclinic.com/health/herbal-treatment-for-anxiety/AN01803

Article: Anxiety and Fears
http://raisingchildren.net.au/articles/anxiety_and_fears.html

Article: No More Panic
http://www.nomorepanic.co.uk/showthread.php?t=27550

Article: Pediatric Generalized Anxiety Disorder Medication
http://emedicine.medscape.com/article/916933-medication

Rational Emotive Therapy :
http://en.wikipedia.org/wiki/Rational_Emotive_Behavior_Therapy

Meditation Oasis Website for Information and Select Meditations:
http://www.meditationoasis.com

Article: Guided Imagery
http://www.Livestrong.com/article/164001-visualization-guided-imagery/

Other Books and E-Books in Dr. T's Living Well Series:

"Overcoming Anger in Teens and Pre-Teens: A Parent's Guide"

"Overcoming Trauma and Loss in Teens and Pre-Teens: A Parent's Guide"

"Overcoming Drug and Alcohol Problems in Teens and Pre-Teens: A Parent's Guide"

"Overcoming Self-Esteem Problems in Teens and Pre-Teens: A Parent's Guide"

"Overcoming ADHD in Teens and Pre-Teens: A Parent's Guide"

"Overcoming Obesity in Teens and Pre-Teens: A Parent's Guide"

"Overcoming Depression in Teens and Pre-Teens: A Parent's Guide"

"Sexual Identity? Moving from Confusion to Clarity"

"Guided Imagery"

"Gay Men's Guide to Love and Relationships"

"Validation Addiction: Please Make Me Feel Worthy"

"The Traveling Parent"

"Tech Etiquette: OMG"

"Wing Lion of Babylon"

"Addicted Nurses: Healing the Caregiver"

"Addicted Physicians: Healing the Healer"

"Addicted Pharmacists: Healing the 'Medicine Man'"

If you know of someone else who might benefit by reading this Book, please tell them about it. Please consider writing a Review.

Thank you,

RLT Publishing

Self-Esteem Enhancers.......

These Self-Esteem Enhancers are actually "affirmations" which are deeply rooted in history....

The theory is that we have become programmed by parents, siblings, society, television, the internet, the media, etc., and this programming has led to our attitudes about ourselves and others. This programming is very often negative, leaving us with a negative self-image.

By taking a positive statement, such as a Self-Esteem Enhancer attached, and repeating it for 7 to 21 days, we begin to change that programming. The more we repeat the statement, and the more feeling behind it, the stronger and quicker the results.

Thinking the statement you pick for 10 times each day is okay, saying it out loud 10 times is good, and saying out loud it and writing it 10 times daily is excellent. One way to begin reprogramming yourself is to mentally repeat the Self-Esteem Enhancer as many times as you can during the day when you have a few free minutes.

****

Directions: Say the Self-Esteem Enhancer which you choose, 10 times in the morning just after rising, and 10 times in the evening just before bed for 7 to 21 days. Say it out loud if at all possible. Looking in a mirror while saying it, gives extra power to the activity. Also, the more times you say it, the quicker and more powerful the results. Concentrate on one Self-Esteem Enhancer at a time for best results. Also, don't share your Self-Esteem Enhancer with anyone else, as you don't want any chance of someone's negative thoughts or comments weakening your efforts to make a positive change in yourself. Good Luck and Bon Voyage on your journey to loving yourself more completely……….

My life is a series of choices and I choose only positive and loving interactions with others.

For the next 24 hours I will attract only positive, loving situations.

The negativity of others bounces off me and I remain centered, focused and clear.

I love my mind and my body.

I leave my negative self-image behind me and see only a positive love-filled me.

Others are attracted to my loving, peaceful nature. I radiate contentment.

My loving thoughts chase away all fear.

I easily release all anger in an appropriate way.

I release and let go of any need to feel guilty.

I radiate peace and contentment.

I forgive myself for living in shame and guilt and easily release the need to feel these limiting feelings.

I release those who I feel have limited or victimized me, by understanding, loving and forgiving them.

I choose peace, love and joy as my companions today.

The child within me plays in the moment and experiences freedom and joy.

This is my day to feel peace, love and harmony in all that I say and do.

I deserve to experience peace, love and harmony.

I am worthy of love.

I am honest, open and loving in all that I say and do.

I believe in ME!

I like myself.

I am loveable.

I feel good about myself.

I have faith in myself.

I love myself.

I am confident.

I now accept myself and others exactly as we are.

Every day I grow to love myself more and more.

I believe in myself.

My thoughts are positive and loving, and I am always attracting this in others.

I am beautiful and loveable and have a great deal to share with others.

Every day in every way I grow more and more positive, calmer and at peace with myself.

I am a positive influence in all situations I encounter.

I am lovable and capable.

The child within me finds healthy ways of play and self-expression.

I believe in ME!

I allow myself to relax and be at peace.

I am a positive influence in all situations I encounter.

I am positive and loving.

I am source of great joy and creativity.

Every day I grow to know and accept myself more and more.

I am beautiful and lovable and have a great deal to share with others.

Every day, in every way, I am getting better and better.

Information about the Author:

Dr. Richard Travis is a psychotherapist in Private Practice in South Florida. He received his first Master's Degree at Edinboro University of Pennsylvania in Education. He received his second Master's Degree in Counselor Education at Florida Atlantic University in Boca Raton, Florida. He received his Doctorate in Higher Education/Counseling Psychology at Florida International University in Miami, Florida. He has Specialties in Addictions, including State, National and International certifications. He has worked with several people in the healthcare industry who have been in Addiction Monitoring Programs, and currently facilitates several groups a month with professionals being monitored by state and federal agencies.

Dr. Travis has taught classes with every age level of student in Pennsylvania, Michigan and Florida, including teaching graduate Social Work classes at Florida International University in Miami. He has also published several articles on the website Ezinearticles.com.

An Excerpt from "<u>Overcoming Drug and Alcohol Problems in Teens and Pre-Teens: A Parent's Guide</u>" by Dr. Richard L. Travis

"Why Some Children Start Using Drugs

There is a strange, and yet very commonplace opinion that only children from poor and needy families are at risk to become drug or alcohol addicted. Unfortunately, this is not true, and alcohol or drug abuse depends on different factors, and social status is not the most important one. One of the main reasons why children start abusing drugs is **the environment**. If your kid's friends have alcohol or drug problems and they hang out with bad or troubled teens – there is a great possibility that your child will start doing the same. Living in a rough neighborhood could also lead to problems with drugs and alcohol as well.

Previous family history of substance usage.

If someone in your family is or was abusing drugs and a child witnessed that process – he will consider it to be normal and will likely start taking drugs as well. Also, <u>countless studies have proven the genetic link in terms of addiction.</u> <u>Teenagers with parents, grandparents or other relatives who had a drinking or drug problem are more likely to develop alcoholism themselves.</u>

Conflict at home.

If parents live separately, fight regularly, have recently divorced or do not pay much attention to keeping the family harmonious and together, then their children are influenced by an unhealthy family environment. These children might start abusing drugs and alcohol to self-medicate their pain, while others will do it as an act of rebellion against the parents who are causing them stress."

Made in the USA
Lexington, KY
06 January 2015